Suzie Miller is a multi award-winning playwright, was writer in residence at Sydney's Griffin Theatre 2012, has worked with international directors in five countries and twice been attached to the National Theatre in London with her work developed at the NT Studio development unit. Miller's works include *Caress/Ache* (developed at National Theatre, London, premiering at the new Eternity Playhouse Sydney in 2014); *June* (atyp with Legs on the Wall); *Dust* (Black Swan Theatre Company). *Driving Into Walls* (Perth International Arts Festival 2012 with Barking Gecko Theatre Company, touring to Sydney Opera House then UK in 2013); *The Sacrifice Zone* (Toronto with Theatre Gargantua in 2012 and 2013); *In the Heart of Darby Park* (Oran Mor Theatre, Glasgow in 2013); *Transparency* (premiered with Ransom Theatre, Belfast in 2009); *Sold* (London's Theatre 503 in 2011); *Reasonable Doubt* (Edinburgh Fringe Festival and NY Fringe Festival in 2008); *All the Blood and All the Water* (Riverside Theatre); *Cross Sections* (TRS and Sydney Opera House); *Confused Sea Conditions* (Philadelphia US April 2009; Sydney 2008); *Flight/ Fright Mode* (Edinburgh Festival 2009, New Theatre, Sydney 2009; London's Southwark Playhouse 2011).

In 2012 Miller was on creative attachment, working with Robert Lepage and Ex Machina in Quebec City on *Playing Cards*.

Miller's awards include the 2008 National Kit Denton Fellowship for writing with courage; shortlisted 2010 and 2005 Australian Writers Guild Award for drama; shortlisted Griffin Award 2009; winner Inscription 2009; and 2006; mentored by Edward Albee 2009; winner 2008 New York Fringe Festival 'Overall Excellence Award for Outstanding Playwriting' and 2005 winner Theatrelab award.

For the wonderful Robert, Gabriel and Sasha

TRANSPARENCY

SUZIE MILLER

CURRENCY PLAYS

First published in 2013
by Currency Press Pty Ltd,
PO Box 2287, Strawberry Hills, NSW, 2012, Australia
enquiries@currency.com.au
www.currency.com.au

NATIONAL LIBRARY OF AUSTRALIA CIP DATA

Author:	Miller, Suzie, author.
Title:	Transparency / Suzie Miller.
ISBN:	9780868199702 (paperback)
Dewey Number:	A822.3

Front cover shows Richard Dormer as Simon in the 2009 Ransom Theatre production (Photo: Rosie Mac Photography). Back cover shows Ed Wightman as Lachlan and Glenn Hazeldine as Simon in the 2011 Seymour Centre production (Photo: Helen White). Cover design by Katy Wall for Currency Press.

Transparency was created with assistance from the Commonwealth Government through the Australia Council, its arts funding and advisory body.

Contents

Currency Press acknowledges the Traditional Owners of the Country on which we live and work. We pay our respects to all Aboriginal and Torres Strait Islander Elders, past and present.

Dorothea Myer-Bennett as Jessica and Richard Dormer as Simon in the 2009 Ransom Theatre production. (Photo: Rosie Mac Photography.)

INTRODUCTION

When I first read *Transparency* I was sure that the playwright, Suzie Miller, had taken some artistic license in fashioning a riveting, multi-level 'who-dunnit' type story. It seemed unfathomable to me that someone could be forced to pay for a childhood crime, albeit horrific, for the rest of their lives through an enforced and effective removal of their past. This seemed to me a punishment that far outweighed the crime. But I was quick to learn that this is indeed a reality for some individuals who, like Simon, Miller's protagonist, have committed the ultimate crime as children.

This element of 'discovery' of a new and very bleak world was one of the reasons I selected *Transparency* to be the Seymour Centre's first full-produced theatre production. As part of the University of Sydney it seemed appropriate that our self-produced productions fed into the University's culture of informed enquiry, of asking important questions. And Miller's play is filled with questions.

Transparency asks us to consider, in detail, how to appropriately rehabilitate those who commit terrible crimes as children. Simon, like others and most notably those who murdered James Bulger, on release from prison must live a life under a new identity to protect his future, those around him and his family from his past. Yet in Act One as Simon, in anguish, begs his counselor for permission to tell the truth to his wife, we see his pain and wonder if this process of rehabilitation is the right one.

Simon's journey through the play is not unlike that of John Proctor in Arthur's Miller's classic, *The Crucible*. For Proctor the prospect of losing his name, of contributing to a fundamental lie is a bridge too far and he chooses death as the preferable alternative. In *Transparency*, Simon has been forced to live a lie for many years and whilst his truth is one many would not want revealed, his inner torment can still be attributed to the pain of living a kind of rootless, nameless life. In Suzie Miller's play Simon carries forward the fundamental question posed in *The Crucible* and, indeed, the hero's journey in many classics. The question of, *who am I?*

At the end of *Transparency*, as in *The Crucible*, both characters achieve a sense of being cleansed through adhering, ultimately, to truth. In Arthur Miller's play we have no doubt that this action was the right thing for Proctor to do; as Elizabeth says, 'He have his goodness now. God forbid I take it from him!' However, in *Transparency* questions remain, leaving the audience in a kind of limbo. We are unsure how his wife, Jessica, will ultimately deal with Simon's truth and the future for Simon is not easy to see. Yet this ambiguity is one of the plays strengths. Ultimately Suzie Miller asks the audience, at the end of the play, to sit with the dilemma and ask ourselves, what would we do in the same circumstance? Given the contemporary nature of the story this leads to the next question: are we as a responsible society actually attempting to rehabilitate individuals such as Simon or simply condemning them to a life sentence?

Indeed *Transparency* is a play of questions.

It is also about betrayal and retribution.

I was surprised that in one of the early performances, an audience member placed the greatest betrayal not on Simon for keeping the woman he loves unaware of his criminal past, but on Jessica for attempting to open Simon's private suitcase—a bag that may contain some clues to his increasingly difficult behaviour. Jessica is on a mission to almost force her husband to be more 'open' despite his protestations. Her gut tells her that something is deeply wrong and she is prepared to go against his wishes to prove herself right. This small transgression, for some, was seen as more deceitful than Simon's far more complex lie. Indeed, many felt that Simon was the most transparent or honest of all the characters in the play.

Lies and betrayal extend throughout the fabric of Miller's other characters: Camille, Simon's co-worker, is trapped in an unsatisfactory marriage but rather than face the prospect of divorce she takes a lover, betraying her husband and child, and creating an ever-increasing web of lies.

Of course, Jessica experiences the greatest betrayal when she finally learns her husband's truth. And this was another reason I wanted to do the play. When we reach the final scenes where, inevitably, we must hear the full details of Simon's crime, Miller's language becomes more disconnected, tangential, visceral and poetic.

Most audiences felt the dilemma in the gut, as Jessica does, defying a logical, analytical response. The play reaches a kind of emotion-filled horror where the language helps us empathise with Jessica's desire to physically hurt Simon and to embrace him at the same time. I was equally confronted by these sections when I first read them and felt that the complex issues that Miller's language raised were good reason to produce the work.

Lachlan, Camille's husband, takes swift retribution ending his marriage with Camille and taking their child with him. Simon's ultimate retribution is somewhat left in the air. We know the retribution he has suffered as part of his sentence but his exact punishment from Jessica and from the wider community remains uncertain—though we know that it could mean a return to prison. Once again Miller turns the ultimate question on us, the audience, asking if, perhaps, this man has suffered enough—questions again.

Producing and directing *Transparency* was enormously satisfying because it is a play that provokes discussion—audiences were captivated and sometimes appalled, but wanted to talk about it afterwards. Points of view varied wildly. Some were adamant that Jessica had no choice but to leave him, endorsing what Andy, Simon's pragmatic counselor, states early in the play as a major threat: *if you tell her, she'll leave.* Others, like me, liked to believe that it was possible that their love was strong enough to somehow steer a course through the betrayal. After all, all Simon has done is tell the truth and it cannot get any worse.

And so, lastly, the play is also about trust: what we choose to tell in a relationship and what not to tell; about the risks we take in confessing truth to those we love—and the trust we must have in them to continue loving us for who we truly are.

Timothy Jones
April 2013

Timothy Jones is Artistic Director and General Manager of the Seymour Centre, Sydney.

Transparency was first produced by the Ransom Theatre Company at the Old Museum Arts Centre (OMAC) Theatre, Belfast, Northern Ireland on 26 September 2009, with the following cast:

SIMON	Richard Dormer
JESSICA	Dorothea Myer-Bennett
CAMILLE	Abigal McGibbon
LACHLAN	Richard Clements
ANDY	Alexandra Ford

All other roles were played by the company.

Director, Rachel O'Riordan
Assistant Director, Patsy Hughes
Designer, Stuart Marshall
Lighting Designer, James Whiteside
Sound Designer, Ashley Martin-Smyth
Stage Manager / Production Manager, Lisa-Marie Cooke

Transparency was first produced in Australia by The Seymour Centre at the York Thetre, Seymour Centre, Sydney, on 1 September 2011, with the following cast:

SIMON	Glenn Hazeldine
JESSICA	Amy Matthews
CAMILLE	Anna Lise Phillips
LACHLAN	Ed Wightman
ANDY	Celia Ireland

Director, Tim Jones
Designer, Stephen Curtis
Lighting Designer, Verity Hampson
Sound Designer, Jeremy Silver
Stage Manager, Katrina McKenzie

PLAYWRIGHT'S NOTES

While writing any play requires a grappling with humanity, the research for *Transparency* shook me to the core. Talking to perpetrators, victims and the families of victims meant I was up close and personal to crimes that were for me deeply disturbing. During this confronting process it became impossible not to be outraged by hideous deeds as well as deeply confused with how a child could commit them. Were they born with some evil trait or did something go terribly wrong? While the narrative of *Transparency* explores these issues through the personal lives of characters, I found it interesting to meditate on the nature of rehabilitation and punishment. Should child criminals be considered forever dangerous or is there hope? What can we trust and what is too great a risk?

Indeed issues of trust and love are interwoven with elements of crime and punishment, and I found myself also questioning: are secrets sometimes better left alone amidst love or is the need for disclosure somehow an act of true intimacy? Do you have to know everything about your lover to maintain your love, and can you ever really know another person entirely anyway?

THANK YOU

I owe a debt of gratitude to the following people and organisations: Robert, Gabriel and Sasha Beech-Jones, Andrew Denton, the Kit Denton Fellowship Award, Tim Jones, Rachel O'Riordan, Timothy Daly, Camilla Rountree, Caleb Lewis, the National Theatre in London, the cast of the National Theatre read, the Seymour Centre, the University of Sydney, Paul O'Beirne and Currency Press, Ransom Theatre UK, Riverside Theatre Australia, and the entire casts of the premier productions. I would also like to thank Hilary Bonney, Lisa Cahill, Rochelle Zurnamer, Celia Ireland, Lucy Bell, Hilary Bell, Karen O'Connell, Rick Goldberg, Julia Pincus, Ian Learmonth, Heather Mitchell, the entire Miller family and the wonderful friends I have who continuously support me in both my theatre career and my life generally.

CHARACTERS

SIMON, works for the National Parks and Wildlife.

JESSICA, married to Simon. Fast, arty, unconventional. Works as a radiography technician at the town hospital.

CAMILLE, Simon's co-worker. Married to Lachlan. She has a two-year-old son, Angus.

LACHLAN, married to Camille. Father to Angus.

ANDY, a government-appointed psychologist.

SETTING

The action takes place in a small town situated near a national park. This story is set over a Christmas period. Should it be staged in the northern hemisphere the author permits appropriate weather conditions to be changed where they are mentioned in the script.

A NOTE ON THE TEXT

A backslash [/] at the end of a line of dialogue indicates the following line immediately runs after this line.

A backslash [/] within the dialogue indicates the next line of dialogue begins, running over or drowning out the remainder of the original line.

An em-dash [—] indicates an unfinished throught, or a moment in which a character doesn't voice their thought. It can also be an interrupted unfinished thought.

ACKNOWLEDGEMENTS

This play has been developed by the National Theatre in London culminating in an industry read in 2009. It has been further developed by Ransom Theatre (new writing theatre) in Belfast. The playwright acknowledges the generous support of the Kit Denton Fellowship awarded for Writing with Courage (2008) for the development of this work; and Playwriting Australia for funds to travel to the National Theatre and Ransom Theatre for the development. The playwright also acknowledges dramaturgy by Timothy Daly and Rachel O'Riordan. O'Riordan has been fundamental to the writing of this work.

ACT ONE

SCENE ONE

An evening in December.

Lead up to Christmas.

Simon and Jessica's place.

A large X-ray collage covers the wall.

Lights up on a radio, illuminated on a kitchen benchtop.

A retro formica table in the centre of the kitchen.

A radio plays sexy music in the background.

SIMON *and* JESSICA *are up against the kitchen wall, in a heated sexual moment.*

JESSICA: God I love your arms.
    And I love your neck.
    And I love your cock.

      Silence as they move together.

    And I love your name.
    I love your beautiful fucking name.

SIMON:—

JESSICA: A name like honey.
    Sticky.
    Burnt honey.

SIMON:—

JESSICA: I want our babies to have your name, our name!

      SIMON *traces her face, her neck.*

SIMON: You're so beautiful Jess.

    She laughs and lets him look over her lovingly, hungrily.

    How did I ever get so lucky?

JESSICA: [*teasing*] Indeed?

They get hotter.

And hotter.

Have to—
Be quick—
Lachlan and Camille will be here soon—

SIMON *groans.*

You love them.

SIMON: I see Camille every day at work.

JESSICA: They're our best friends.

SIMON: I just want you.

JESSICA: I just want your arms!

SIMON: [*teasing*] So you fell in love with me because of my arms?

JESSICA: No, because of your name.
Saw your beautiful name on the list.
First thing I loved!

SIMON *stops briefly.*

SIMON: What if I was called... Tobias?

JESSICA: [*joking, flirting*] I'd be fucking Tobias right now!

SIMON: Jesus Jess.

JESSICA: As long as he had your arms, your neck, your cock!
Your fucking arms.

SIMON *is disconcerted, and hesitates.*

Hey.
Idiot.
It's not just—
It's you.
The all of you.

He stares at her, transfixed.

We would make a beautiful baby.

SIMON:—

JESSICA: [*playfully*] Try saying 'Yes Jess, one day we will make a beautiful baby'.

Amy Mathews as Jessica and Glenn Hazeldine as Simon in the 2011
Seymour Centre production. (Photo: Helen White.)

She kisses him passionately.

The energy becomes more intense.

Hotter.

They'll be here soon.

JESSICA *takes his hands and holds her own above her head.*

SIMON *snatches them down and tries to be gentle, romantic.*

JESSICA *is more urgent, more demanding, with whispered encouragement.*

She resists SIMON*'s gentleness and insists with her body on ramping up the energy, repeatedly trying to get him to hold her against the wall.*

God I love you.
SIMON: I love *you.*

She grabs him and takes him to the floor /table where her desire for him to do things her way is obvious from her insistent actions.

He doesn't at first but then as things hot up, he starts to follow her lead.

JESSICA: [*she puts her hands and arms back coquettishly*] Hold me so I can't get my arms down.
No not like that.
Tighter.

SIMON *does so, taking control*

JESSICA *enjoys the feeling of being held down, wants to lose herself to it.*

SIMON:—
JESSICA: That's it.

SIMON *holds her down, putting his weight against her.*

He starts to sexually lose himself, starts to enjoy it.

Harder. Restrain me honey.

He looks into her face and pulls away suddenly.

Drops hold of her, and leaves her lying on the table /floor.

JESSICA *is dishevelled, confused.*

SIMON: No. I can't.

Awkward moment but then JESSICA *tickles him.* SIMON *pulls away.*

Don't. Please don't.

JESSICA: What?

Beat.

Hold me baby, hold me tightly.

[*Teasing*] Mr Simon Font-aine. Font-aine. Fontaine.

SIMON: Don't. Don't. And stop the name stuff.

JESSICA:—?

SIMON: I don't hold people down.

I don't do 'restraint'.

JESSICA *laughs, thinking this is part of the game.*

She goes to grab him and pull him down.

He pushes her away.

This is not negotiable.

She is shocked and confused.

Awkwardness.

She tries to cover herself up.

You think I want to hurt you?

JESSICA: [*hotly and defensively*] No.

It was just play.

God.

SIMON:—

They both start to put on their clothes.

JESSICA *starts to clean up the kitchen.*

Starts to cry.

SIMON: Jess.
Please—

She won't look at him.

I'm sorry.
Don't cry.
Please don't cry.
JESSICA: It's humiliating.

He tries to embrace her but she resists.

By this stage they are both fully dressed.

An awkward silence.

SIMON: Tell me why.
Restraining you.
You think I'd want—?
To you?
JESSICA: Because I asked you to.
Because we can.
Because I feel safe.
Because it's you.

Silence.

In the silence there is a connectedness between them.

A short time passes before the voice over interrupts this silence.

CAMILLE: [*voiceover*] Hello.
It's us!

Beat.

JESSICA: Door's open.

JESSICA *wipes her eyes.*

SIMON *and* JESSICA *are forced to change the mood as* CAMILLE *enters, carrying a bottle of champagne.*

CAMILLE: Lachlan's carrying the sleeping child to your bedroom.
JESSICA: Yes.
Good idea.

Beat.

CAMILLE: Champagne!

SIMON *takes it from her.*

CAMILLE: For the celebration.

SIMON: Wow champagne. Thanks Camille.

Beat.

LACHLAN *enters.* SIMON *is pouring drinks and handing them out.*

LACHLAN: He's out like a light!

SIMON: [*nodding*] Lachlan.

LACHLAN: Hi Simon!

LACHLAN *is struck by the huge collage on the wall. He whistles.*

So here it is?

JESSICA: Here it is!

LACHLAN *studies the wall.*

LACHLAN: So which bits are you,
And which bits are Simon?

CAMILLE: Jesus Lachlan it doesn't matter.

JESSICA: It's random.
That's the point—a merging of us!
[*To* SIMON] Happy First Anniversary babe.

SIMON *looks over at her.*

LACHLAN: Um. Jess you know I think you're amazing—
But I just. Don't.
I don't get it.

CAMILLE: There's nothing to get.
It's a [*She makes air inverted commas*] 'collage'.

LACHLAN: I know that!

CAMILLE: Jess is a radi-og-rapher! /

LACHLAN: Yeah. Duh!

CAMILLE: [*laughing*] 'Duh'! I haven't heard that word in ages!

JESSICA: It's—
Kind of our story, isn't it, Simon?

SIMON: We met over / my broken arm.

CAMILLE: Your broken arm.

And the way he looked at her /

JESSICA: Broke my heart open!

LACHLAN: How'd you break it?

JESSICA: My heart!? /

LACHLAN: His arm.

CAMILLE: Lachlan loves detail.

JESSICA: Sign of a competent journalist.

LACHLAN: [*to* CAMILLE] Yes.

Thanks Jess.

JESSICA: I X-rayed both his arms.

The broken one and the healthy one. /

SIMON: I couldn't understand why!

JESSICA: I wanted to keep you there longer!

CAMILLE: [*sarcastically*] Romantic.

LACHLAN: Come on. It is!

You love it Camille, admit it.

She looks at him as he moves towards the collage.

Is this Simon's leg?

JESSICA: No, that's my femur, and his tibia, and look—

That's the rib area around my heart.

Spine.

And that's my bottom!

LACHLAN: And a beautiful X-rayed bottom it is too.

SIMON: Just scans herself at work,

when she's bored.

CAMILLE: Jesus!

JESSICA: All the technicians do!

LACHLAN: Is it safe?

I mean if you're trying for a baby.

SIMON: We're not.

LACHLAN: But I thought—

JESSICA stops him with a look.

Silence. LACHLAN *changes the subject.*

Uh... I've been assigned that missing toddler story.
JESSICA: Shit.
CAMILLE: How old is he?
LACHLAN: Just two. Denis Pritchard.
JESSICA: They still haven't found him?
SIMON: A missing child?
LACHLAN: You haven't heard?

SIMON *shakes his head.*

JESSICA: There's a huge search.
LACHLAN: Cops are all over it.
JESSICA: How does a kid go missing here?
LACHLAN: They think he might have wandered off into the bush,
    Or that someone might have snatched him.
JESSICA: It's so awful.
CAMILLE: [*to* SIMON] If the police don't find him by Friday Matt will
    have us both working on the weekend
LACHLAN: This weekend?
CAMILLE:—
LACHLAN: Matt's pushing his luck
CAMILLE: If I'm needed I'm needed, Lachlan.
LACHLAN: [*sarcastically*] Hmm.
JESSICA: Camille you sound like my husband.
LACHLAN: The job is everything! /
CAMILLE: Come on it's a missing child. /
JESSICA: God it's so hot out there!
    He'll be so dehydrated.
LACHLAN: They have to find him within 96 hours or I don't know—
CAMILLE: Which is why if we're called in to work /
JESSICA: Oh God... ?
CAMILLE: It's so secluded in the bush.
    No-one would even hear him out there.
SIMON: [*loudly*] Please.

    Beat.

    Can we talk about something else?
JESSICA: Why would the mother leave him alone in the garden?
    Even for five minutes.

CAMILLE: Any parent could. /
LACHLAN: I wouldn't.

>   *A slightly awkward moment.*

>   [*Gently*] And neither would you, darling.
CAMILLE: I might have!
JESSICA: It must be awful for you
>   Reporting on it, thinking about it
>   With Angus nearly the same age and /
LACHLAN: He was playing in the studio
>   While I read the police reports on air!
JESSICA: [*shuddering*] How do you cope?
LACHLAN: Well it would be quite nice to have my wife *home on the weekends.*

>   *Uncomfortable silence.*

>   LACHLAN *looks at a bruise on* SIMON*'s arm.*

Nasty bruise there Simon.

>   SIMON *pulls away his arm.*

SIMON: I did it playing squash
JESSICA: [*to* SIMON] You should take Lachie to squash with you and Andy.
SIMON: Lachlan doesn't play squash.
LACHLAN: Well not yet.
CAMILLE: Lachie can pretty much do anything he puts his mind to.
LACHLAN: Thanks honey.

>   CAMILLE *shrugs, it wasn't actually a compliment.*

JESSICA: Go on.
>   I'll babysit Angus.
CAMILLE: Jess I can look after him.
JESSICA: Yes yes, of course.

>   *Beat.*

>   LACHLAN *hugs* CAMILLE.

LACHLAN: Great.
>   [*To* SIMON] So it's all sorted. When do we play?

SIMON: I don't—
      There's not enough court time for three of us.
      [*To* LACHLAN] I will play another time with you.
JESSICA: They're very competitive.
      You should see Simon's face when he's lost!
LACHLAN: Or we could play doubles with my mate Dave—he plays at
      the same courts.
      Said he saw you there with your beautiful wife the other day.
JESSICA: I've never been there.
LACHLAN: Really?!
JESSICA: Yeah, it's an hour's drive away!
      So who's the mystery girl there then?
SIMON: I have no idea.

      She punches him playfully.

JESSICA: Hey let's ask Andy to the hospital Christmas party.
SIMON: Andy's just a squash mate.
JESSICA: He never comes to anything.
CAMILLE: Is he good looking?
      —
      My sister's single.
JESSICA: I don't know, I've never met him.
      Is he Simon?
SIMON: Ask Matt to come, he's single.
CAMILLE: No.
      He's not for my sister.
JESSICA: He's gorgeous. /
CAMILLE: Not her type.
      And I don't want to mix work and home.
JESSICA: It's Christmas—perfect time to mix work and home!
      In fact—Simon…
SIMON: What?
JESSICA: I kind of volunteered you!
LACHLAN: Uh oh.
SIMON: For what?
JESSICA: If it's alright with you.
      You don't have to—

SIMON: What is it?!

JESSICA: The usual guy is away—
And I know you're a little bit young, but with the costume—

SIMON: What are you talking about?

JESSICA: We all agreed the kids'll love you.

She starts humming a playful 'Santa Claus is Coming to Town'.

LACHLAN *smiles and it dawns on* SIMON.

SIMON: No.

JESSICA: [*laughing, thinking he doesn't mean it*] Thanks, you're a sweetie.

SIMON: No.

JESSICA: What?

SIMON: No.
I can't do it.

JESSICA: You'll be gorgeous babe.
Anyway it's good practice... /

LACHLAN: For parenthood.

JESSICA: Yeah!

Brief awkwardness.

LACHLAN: Which I can highly recommend by the way.
Parenthood.

CAMILLE: [*almost under her breath*] Yeah.
Of course you can.

LACHLAN: Hey I heard that. You recommend it too, honey.

CAMILLE *looks at him deadpan.*

JESSICA: So Santa!

SIMON: No love.
You'll have to find someone else.

JESSICA: But I volunteered you—

LACHLAN: Can't be a scrooge at Christmas time. /

SIMON: So you do it.

LACHLAN: Well I would but /—

CAMILLE: You're looking after Angus

Beat.

Amy Mathews as Jessica and Anna Lise Phillips as Camille in the 2011 Seymour Centre production. (Photo: Helen White.)

JESSICA: [*to* SIMON] You'll look really handsome with that white
   beard.

SIMON: No Jessica.

JESSICA: But /—

SIMON: I said no!

SCENE TWO

Later.

SIMON *stares at his trunk.*

He is visibly distressed and anxious.

He stands there, staring at it.

JESSICA: [*offstage*] Simon.
   Simon.
   Where are you?
   Are you here?
   Simon!

   SIMON *turns toward the voice of* JESSICA.

SCENE THREE

Squash court.

SIMON *and* ANDY *are playing squash.*

SIMON *misses a ball.*

SIMON: Dammit. Eleven all.
   I dunno—
   It's just getting so difficult.
   I just want to tell her.
   Something.
   Just something small even.

   ANDY, *a woman, comes into view as she runs across the court
   to hit a ball.*

ANDY: You can't.

SIMON: She's talking about babies!

ANDY: You can't tell her anything.

SIMON: So…

You're the only one who can really know me?

Is that it?

ANDY: We've been through this, Simon.

SIMON: I thought you wanted me to be a man in the world

Not some eternally fucked-up teenager?

ANDY: Simon, I know you're a man.

I know that man.

SIMON: You like having power over me, don't you?

He slams the ball.

Did you hear a little boy disappeared?

ANDY: Yes.

SIMON:—

He slams the ball hard.

ANDY: What's going on Simon? /

SIMON: I'm just sick of always doing everything your way.

ANDY: Is that how you see it? 'My way'?

SIMON: Shit.

Game Ball Match.

ANDY: Okay so tell her everything.

Is that what you want me to say?

SIMON: No. I—

Moment.

ANDY: Watch the ball Simon.

SIMON: I am watching the fucking ball.

He loses another point.

ANDY: Fowl. Score.

And stops.

Pause.

SIMON: I love her so much but—

I just don't want to lose her.

She asked me to—

Hold her down. /
ANDY: Hold her down!?
Beat.
SIMON: It scared me.

SCENE FOUR

Sound of radio tuning. LACHLAN *either reads the announcement, wearing earphones, or talks into a dictaphone.*

LACHLAN: The entire district continues to be on alert following the suspicious disappearance of two-year-old Denis Pritchard. Little Denis was last seen playing in his back garden. His mother, Ms Pritchard, raised the alarm. Ms Jane Pritchard, the boy's single mother, raised the alarm. Authorities are looking to inform the child's biological father of the emergency.

Police are continuing an intensive search, but say his safety is cause for grave concern.

This is Lachlan Cooper reporting for Radio 6.

LACHLAN *removes his earphones and the next scene begins.*

SCENE FIVE

LACHLAN *and* CAMILLE *at home.*

He enters the room where CAMILLE *is just sitting.*

LACHLAN: He's just gone down.
Eyes closed almost before I lay him in the cot.
CAMILLE: I would have done it.
LACHLAN: What hon?
CAMILLE: Got him to sleep.
LACHLAN: Of course you would have,
You're doing great with him.
Silence.

They both know this is a lie.
You look tired.

CAMILLE: No actually.
   Not at all.
LACHLAN: Why don't you call a friend and catch a movie?
CAMILLE: You want me out of your way!?
LACHLAN: God Camille, I was being nice.
CAMILLE: Really?
   It doesn't feel that way.
LACHLAN: For God's sake
   Most parents would leap at the chance to /
CAMILLE: So come with me.
   To the movies.
LACHLAN: We can't get a sitter without notice.
CAMILLE: I'll see if Jess'll do it.

   She picks up her phone, looks like she is dialling.

LACHLAN: No I'd better not.
   Angus is too sick.
CAMILLE: Hardly. He's just a bit sniffly.
   Anyway we all know Jess would cope fine if he is.
LACHLAN: I'll just stay here with him.
CAMILLE: Right!
LACHLAN: 'Right' what?
CAMILLE: You managed to make it to work today though.

   Beat while LACHLAN *ignores her.*

Didn't you?

   Beat.

   LACHLAN *stands, shakes his head, and picks up some notes before leaving.*

SCENE SIX

The next day.

SIMON *is squatting before his trunk.*

He places some clothes from a sports bag into it.

JESSICA *arrives.*

JESSICA: What are you doing here in the cold?
SIMON: What are you doing?
JESSICA: I came to find my husband /
SIMON: To spy on him? /
JESSICA: What? No. /
SIMON: You sure? /
JESSICA: Why would I want to spy on you? /
SIMON: Pad pad pad.
    Like a little minxy cat.
JESSICA: Simon!
    I live here too.
SIMON:—
JESSICA: What's in the trunk?
SIMON: It's just personal stuff.
JESSICA: Photos? Documents?
    Things from your mum and stepdad?
SIMON: It's just stuff.
JESSICA: You never—
    Do you miss them?
    Your family?
SIMON: No.
JESSICA: Simon, I think we need our own little family.

    He kisses her.

SIMON: You know I'm not the baby type.
JESSICA: I think you are the baby type!

    He shrugs.

SIMON: Let's go inside.
JESSICA: Are you okay?

    He nods.

SIMON: I'm hungry.

    They embrace.

SCENE SEVEN

SIMON *and* ANDY *at the squash courts.*

At a table after the game. She sits, he paces.

SIMON: I'm confused.
    Why so often?
ANDY: Because I believe you need to see me this much right now.
SIMON: Oh.
    Do I?
ANDY: Yes.
SIMON: Because it's the holiday period or—
    So you can stop me telling Jess stuff?
ANDY: No, so I can provide the support you need.
    And Simon you made a commitment.
    You have to honour that.
SIMON:—
ANDY: You could lose everything.
SIMON: And so could you.
ANDY: Don't threaten me, Simon.
SIMON: If I fuck up then your great rehabilitation theory
    Is dead in the water. /
ANDY: I won't let you fuck up.
SIMON: What do you care, Andy?
ANDY: Care?
    I've been your state-appointed therapist
    For over ten years.
SIMON: You get paid to care.
ANDY: No.
SIMON: Yes.
ANDY: Yes but—
    Look I travel two hours from the city to see you.
    I come here once a week.
    You wanted me here I agreed. I didn't have to.
    No office.
    Squash game so you can minimise eye contact.
    Simon I've done all that for you and I am not sure that everyone
    would agree with my decision.

Brief silence.

I care.

Beat.

SIMON: Okay. So, I trust you.

But—

But if I don't—

If I don't give her something

I'll lose her.

ANDY: Don't throw your life away.

SIMON: Which life should I not throw away?

ANDY: You're being provocative.

Beat.

If you value the life you have.

Don't tell her.

SIMON: She said she fell in love with my fucking name.

ANDY: So?

SIMON: Just let me tell her my first name?

ANDY: Simon no!

Beat.

You know your reintegration depends on you maintaining your new identity.

SIMON: But you get to know it all.

Every tiny detail.

You own more of me than I do.

ANDY: That's just the consequence of my role.

SIMON: Is it?

Or is it just that you like it like this?

ANDY: Don't play this game with me.

SIMON: Game!

ANDY: Simon, you have a good government job, a good relationship, a home /—

SIMON: I want her.

ANDY: You have her.

SIMON: I want her to know me.

ANDY: I know you!

SIMON: That doesn't count.

ANDY: Jessica knows the new you!

SIMON: I need to know if she would still want me, understand me, love me, if she knew everything.

ANDY: She would leave.

SIMON:—

ANDY: I'm warning you.

Don't step outside the world you've created. /

SIMON: You created.

ANDY: No. Simon.

You did this.

You know I want you to succeed.

And that I trust you.

SIMON: You trust me?

ANDY: I do.

SIMON: Then why in all these years nothing?

I know nothing about your life.

ANDY: I trust you Simon.

SIMON: Prove it.

Tell me.

Something.

Anything.

ANDY:—

SIMON: What's your husband's name? /

ANDY: We've spoken about this, Simon.

SIMON: He talk to you like I do, Andy?

Tell you everything?

ANDY: Don't. /

SIMON: No I didn't think so.

So tell me Andy.

What's his name?

ANDY:—

SIMON: You're scared I'm going to track him down and shoot him.

Strangle him with my bare arms.

Is that your trust?

ANDY: No.

There have to be boundaries.

Pause.

SIMON: You have kids, don't you, Andy?

Beat.

ANDY: No.

SIMON: If you did
Would you let me meet them?
Leave me alone with them?

ANDY:—

SIMON: A boy went missing.

ANDY: I know.
Denis Pritchard.

SIMON: A two-year-old.
Vulnerable age.
Age where they'll just hold your hand and go.
No sense of evil,
Just trusting little souls.

ANDY: It's unnerving for you.

SIMON: And not for you?
Okay so you don't have kids
But... if you did would you even tell me?

ANDY:—

SIMON: What if I didn't think it was working with us any longer?
I'd have to ask for someone else, a new therapist.

Beat.

ANDY: Michael.

SIMON: What?

ANDY: My husband's name. Michael.

SCENE EIGHT

SIMON *arrives home with his squash racquet.*

JESSICA *sits at the table reading a flyer about the missing boy.*

JESSICA: Who won?

SIMON: Me.

JESSICA: [*loudly and accusatory*] Liar.

SIMON:—?

JESSICA: [*laughing*] You'd be more excited if you'd won!

> *He looks at the flyer she is reading.*

SIMON: What are these for?

JESSICA: We're handing them out at the hospital.
To help with the search.
It's nearly three days now,
Someone has to know something.
Camille left a message for you.
They're searching the area.
Tomorrow.
You don't think they're looking for / a—?

SIMON: I need a shower.

JESSICA: Christ, imagine if you found him.
Out there,
Dead.

SIMON: Can we not
Talk about it.

JESSICA: So let me in more. You bottle things up honey.

SIMON: It's the only way I know, Jess.

> *He wraps his arms around her, and then releases her as she goes to pour drinks for them both.*

JESSICA: I have a feeling I know what would help.
Fill in the last gap.

> SIMON *looks confused.*

All these parents at Christmas time.
Hanging up Santa sacks.

SIMON: No Jess, not this again.

JESSICA: Babies make people even closer.

SIMON: Not always.

JESSICA: I know we say 'one day'.
But—A baby by next Christmas?

SIMON: Jess.

> *He takes hold of her.*

I just don't know if I can ever do it.

JESSICA: But you'd do it for me, wouldn't you?

SIMON:—

JESSICA: Or is it like the Christmas party?

SIMON: Jess!

JESSICA: Are you saying you wouldn't do it for me?

SIMON: What? Dress up as Santa or have a baby?

JESSICA: Both.

SIMON: I don't want to.

JESSICA: What? Have a baby or dress up as Santa?

SIMON:—

JESSICA: They said to thank you so much.

At work.

SIMON: Please Jess, ask someone else.

JESSICA: I'm asking you.

SIMON: I can't. /

JESSICA: Why?

SIMON:—

JESSICA: Well?

SIMON: Why are you putting me in this position?

JESSICA: What position?

SIMON: You're turning everything around,

Twisting things.

Unravelling /—

JESSICA: Unravelling?

Beat.

Simon?

She goes over to him and tries to hold him.

I want a baby boy

Who is just like his dad.

You could teach him to play football. /

SIMON: Can't.

I've never kicked a ball in my life.

JESSICA: What about when you were a kid?

SIMON: Nup.

Hated team sports.

Never went near football.

JESSICA: Yes you did silly.
SIMON: No. Never.

> JESSICA *moves away.*

JESSICA: So are you saying you lied to me?
SIMON:—?
JESSICA: You've never played football?

> JESSICA *holds his eyes a moment, then takes an X-ray off the wall.*

Lied even at our first meeting.
SIMON: What are you talking about?
JESSICA: Your other arm
Your good one.
I X-rayed them both—
Remember?
Three childhood breaks.
You laughed and said it was years of football.
SIMON: No, I said I fell out of a tree.
JESSICA: No you didn't.
SIMON: Yes I did.
JESSICA: And broke you arm in three places?
SIMON: Yes!
JESSICA: On the same fall?
SIMON: I was really high up.

> *She looks at the X-ray then back at* SIMON.

JESSICA: You're lying.
The breaks are at different ages.
Three different occasions.
So if it's not 'years of football' then…

> *He grabs the X-ray from her and tries to stick it back on the wall.*

Three childhood arm breaks. /
SIMON: Okay, maybe it was football but—
I managed to hold you down the other night.
I think my arms are doing fine don't you? /
JESSICA: You're lying.
Someone did this to you, didn't they? /

SIMON: There's this beautiful woman who wants to take pictures of my arm. My busted arm. And as soon as I lay eyes on her I know /...

JESSICA: What happened to you?

Tell me. /

SIMON: Long sexy legs, and even in her hospital uniform, such style.

He goes to try to kiss her, to touch her.

She resists.

JESSICA: Please Simon.

Talk to me.

I need you to share who you are. /

SIMON: The way she moved.

I wanted to have a broken bone every day of my life. /

JESSICA: Simon! /

SIMON: My first, my only love. My soulmate. /

JESSICA: I want to know. /

SIMON: I wanted to fuck you right then and there.

In the hospital.

He tries to get more sexual with her, but JESSICA *is resisting.*

JESSICA: Don't you believe in me enough to tell me?

SIMON:—

He tries to kiss her to stop her talking.

JESSICA: Stop it.

SIMON:—

JESSICA: I need this.

Really need this.

SIMON: Please don't need it.

JESSICA: Tell me.

SIMON:—

JESSICA: Trust me.

Beat.

Me.

SIMON:—

JESSICA: Who did it?

SIMON: No-one.

JESSICA: I. Can. Tell.

Your stepfather.

It was him wasn't it?

SIMON:—

JESSICA: He broke your arm?

SIMON:—

SIMON *is stonewalling her.*

JESSICA: Talk to me. /

SIMON: What do you want?

JESSICA: Tell me about the broken arm.

Your stepfather did it?

SIMON: Yes.

JESSICA: And your mum?

What did she do?

SIMON: Look, I probably provoked him.

JESSICA: Your mum. /

SIMON: Nothing. She did nothing.

JESSICA: She did nothing?

SIMON: Later I got taken away. At ten.

Jess, you can't tell anyone.

Ever.

JESSICA: Where did they take you?

SIMON: I don't know.

JESSICA: Foster home?

SIMON: No. No, a place.

JESSICA: What place?

SIMON: A place they take kids like me.

JESSICA: I can't believe you've never told me.

SIMON: I'm telling you now!

JESSICA: How could they—

How can anyone hurt a child?

SIMON: [*urgently*] Swear to me.

You'll never tell anyone.

JESSICA: Why? You didn't do anything wrong.

You shouldn't have to hide.

SIMON: Jessica, okay listen to me, you can't tell Lachlan or Camille /

JESSICA: They'd understand.

SIMON: No!

Listen to me. /

JESSICA: That mysterious part of you.

This is the key Simon, something clicked /—

SIMON: Jessica you can't talk about this.

He urgently pushes her up against the wall.

Tries to get her to look him in the eyes.

JESSICA: Simon.

SIMON: Don't say anything, okay?

JESSICA: [*calmly*] Simon, you're hurting me.

He immediately lets go. He backs up, hands in the air.

What happened just now?

What was that Simon?

Beat.

SIMON: I'll wear the costume.

JESSICA: What?

SIMON: Santa.

I'll do it.

Okay?

I'll be Santa for you.

SCENE NINE

Noises from a children's playground.

CAMILLE *tries unsuccessfully to unfold the stroller.*

LACHLAN *appears on stage. Angus is playing offstage in the playground sandpit.*

LACHLAN: Daddy's watching Angus.

Daddy's watching.

Good work Angus.

Put some in the bucket.

No no, don't throw the sand.

Naughty naughty—
That's right. In the bucket.

CAMILLE *is still struggling with the stroller.*

LACHLAN *comes and stands by.*

She kicks the stroller.

CAMILLE: It's fucked.
LACHLAN: Language!
CAMILLE: Come on Lachie, it's stuffed.
LACHLAN:—
CAMILLE: No, it really is this time.
LACHLAN: You'll get the hang of it.
Just have another try.
CAMILLE: I.
Can't.
Do.
It.
LACHLAN: It just takes a bit of patience.

CAMILLE *stares at him.*

What?
CAMILLE: Fuck off!

CAMILLE *storms off.*

LACHLAN *wheels the stroller off toward Angus.*

SCENE TEN

SIMON *is in front of his unopened trunk. He runs his hands over it.*

LACHLAN, *in earphones, reads the news announcement.*

LACHLAN: While the hunt continues for missing two-year-old Denis Pritchard, the record temperatures are challenging hopes for a safe recovery. Police helicopters continue to scour the extended areas of bush surrounding the district. Forensic experts have been consulted in an attempt to put together a profile of any possible abductor…

SCENE ELEVEN

SIMON *and* JESSICA *'s place.*

Early evening.

It's the night of JESSICA *'s hospital work Christmas party.*

JESSICA: It's past ninety-six hours.
CAMILLE: Would take a miracle now.
JESSICA: Oh God.
LACHLAN: The police say they have a lead.
CAMILLE: Poor mother must be in living hell for leaving him outside
    alone.
    And with Christmas a few days away—
JESSICA: They're going to have a table at the Christmas party tonight.
    Selling cupcakes to raise money for the family.
CAMILLE: Cupcakes!

    Sound of Angus crying out.

CAMILLE: [*to* LACHLAN] Is that Angus?
LACHLAN: Probably your turn by now.
CAMILLE:—

    Beat.

LACHLAN: Go on then.
CAMILLE: He probably wants you. /
LACHLAN: Camille. You can do it.
    Just go to him. /
CAMILLE: Okay Lachlan.

    CAMILLE *exits.*

LACHLAN: Thanks for inviting us along.
JESSICA:—

    CAMILLE *enters.*

CAMILLE: He's playing.
    Where's Simon?
JESSICA: [*calling out*] Simon.

    SIMON *enters wearing a Santa costume. He is extremely unsure.*

Oh babe, you look fantastic.
LACHLAN: Ho ho ho.
CAMILLE: Oh my God, you're the real thing.
JESSICA: Come on Simon, cheer up!
CAMILLE: Scarily real!
SIMON: Yeah well, Santa's not real is he?
LACHLAN: Maybe not but he sure is grumpy!
JESSICA: Let me get a photo—everyone squash in.
LACHLAN: I'll get Angus?
SIMON: No. No photos Jessica.
    I said no photos.
JESSICA: Are you kidding?
    It's part of the job,
    There won't be a parent there without a camera hon.
CAMILLE: You'll be a kid magnet!
LACHLAN: [*laughing and distracted*] You'll be in paedophile heaven.
SIMON: What the fuck did you say? /
LACHLAN: Mate, I didn't mean /—
JESSICA: Simon, it was just a stupid joke. /
CAMILLE: Simon? Are you okay? /
SIMON: You're in my house.
    And you say something like that to me? /

    SIMON *grabs* LACHLAN.

JESSICA: Fuck Simon! /
CAMILLE: Sime.
JESSICA: Let him go, you're hurting him! /

    SIMON *let's go abruptly and* LACHLAN *falls to the ground.*

    They all watch SIMON *in disbelief. He is freaking out.*

SIMON: I'm sorry. I'm sorry.
    Oh God. I didn't mean to—

    JESSICA *goes to* LACHLAN *on the ground.*

    SIMON *rips off the Santa outfit.*

[*Angrily, to* JESSICA] I told you I couldn't do it.
You wouldn't listen.

I said I didn't want to do this shit and, I fucking don't.

JESSICA: Jesus Simon.

He storms out.

CAMILLE: I'll go catch him up.

She leaves.

LACHLAN: I'm pissing off everyone.

JESSICA: Are you okay?

LACHLAN: Yeah I'm fine.

JESSICA: He looked like he was going to hit you.

LACHLAN: I said something stupid.

JESSICA: He's just not himself.

LACHLAN: He really isn't a Santa fan.

JESSICA: I think he's stressed with work and—
And things with us.
God I'm so sorry.
I mean he's always had his difficult family stuff.
But
This short fuse—
It's a new side to him.

LACHLAN: What do you mean?

JESSICA: Nothing.

LACHLAN: Has he hurt you?

JESSICA: No.

LACHLAN: If he—
I would fucking kill him.

Beat.

JESSICA: I'm fine.
But thanks.

A moment. LACHLAN *looks lovingly at* JESSICA *who is confused and looks away.*

LACHLAN: [*gesturing to her*] Here.

JESSICA: What?

LACHLAN: Give me the suit.

JESSICA: Would you?

Beat.

Oh. Thank you Lachlan. So much.

Imagine having to tell all those little kids there's no Santa coming?

LACHLAN: You'll make a great mum.

JESSICA: I've stopped taking the pill.

I'm really ready for a baby.

In fact—

I think I might—

I'm going for a test at the hospital tomorrow!

LACHLAN: That's great.

JESSICA: I know—

I just hope Simon calms down.

LACHLAN: He will. It's just a one off.

All men can react oddly, even me at times!

JESSICA: Thanks Lachlan.

You won't say anything?

LACHLAN: Does Santa love his Goddam fucking reindeers!

JESSICA *looks down at the discarded costume.*

JESSICA: Well no, it appears he doesn't!

They laugh.

Lach, I haven't told Simon that I've stopped taking the pill.

In case he disagrees about the timing.

LACHLAN: But—

Jess you have to tell him.

A baby changes everything.

JESSICA: I'm not a liar.

It's the only secret I've ever had.

LACHLAN:—

JESSICA: I'm just really ready for a baby and—

Simon wants one, it's just—

I think he's scared.

LACHLAN: You'll be a beautiful mother.

JESSICA: You think so?

Simon's so independent. Like Camille.

But Camille's glad now isn't she? With Angus? She's glad she had him, isn't she?

LACHLAN: I guess—
      She's adjusting.
JESSICA: You don't think I'm being terribly dishonest, do you?
LACHLAN: I think
      Simon is incredibly lucky.
JESSICA: So is Camille.
LACHLAN: You're lovely.
JESSICA: Thanks.
LACHLAN: Really lovely.

He touches her hair.

CAMILLE *walks in, catching the strangely intimate moment.*

LACHLAN *and* JESSICA *jump apart.*

An uncomfortable silence.

CAMILLE: I couldn't catch him. /
JESSICA: Oh, um, Lachlan has offered to be Santa.
CAMILLE: Great.

An uncomfortable silence.

So I guess Lachlan should be getting his kit *on* then. Shouldn't he?

They all look down at the discarded Santa gear.

SCENE TWELVE

JESSICA *tries to open the trunk, but realises it is locked.*

The key can't be found anywhere.

She madly searches, getting increasingly frustrated.

When she realises she can't find the key, she wrestles with the case, then thumps it in defeat.

SCENE THIRTEEN

SIMON *has just arrived at the squash courts.* ANDY *is dressed for squash game,* SIMON *is not.*

ANDY: You're not dressed!

SIMON: No more games.

ANDY: Squash was your idea Simon.

SIMON: That's not my name.

ANDY: Okay so you're testing me.

What's going on Simon?

SIMON: I chose you because you promised.

ANDY: Let's get something straight. You didn't choose me Simon. And there are no promises.

SIMON: You promised me you'd never talk.

> SIMON *takes out the newspaper and waves it around.*

You fucking gave me your word you wouldn't talk /—

ANDY: Okay so I can see you read the newspaper article /—

SIMON: 'Two years old. A vulnerable age, an age when they will just hold your hand and go. No sense of evil.

Just trusting little souls.'

Straight out of my fucking mouth. You quoted me!

ANDY: You're angry.

SIMON: Yes I'm angry!

ANDY: They were doing an article about serious crime and rehabilitation.

They approached me.

Simon I'm an expert in rehabilitation.

SIMON: Everything you know is because of me.

ANDY: No Simon, because of me. Because of my hard work in this field.

SIMON: Things I told you.

ANDY: They were asking me about the missing boy, because they are asking everyone, all experts, about what might have happened.

And eventually someone, an investigating officer, will probably want to talk to you.

SIMON: But I was *ten.*

ANDY: I know that, but you understand /—

SIMON: Ten years old. /

ANDY: It doesn't ever go away. /

SIMON: You think I don't know that.

You think I don't wake up every day knowing—

Hating—

Five minutes when I was ten years old will count forever!

ANDY: That's the reality Simon.

SIMON: You like owning me, don't you Andy?

Why, why do you like it so much?

ANDY: I don't 'own you'.

SIMON: You have other people to talk to.

What about me?

I want to talk to other people too.

You like having me all to yourself.

ANDY: I am part of your program.

SIMON: No.

Stop it.

It's more than that.

You can't let me go.

ANDY: [*slightly less controlled*] No that's not true.

Beat.

SIMON: Please Andy. Please.

Just don't talk to them, the television, newspapers.

Don't keep mentioning what I did.

ANDY: Okay, no-one would ever know it's about you.

You have a new identity,

A whole new history,

Trust me.

You're a wonderful case of rehabilitation,

A success.

SIMON: It's all theory to you, isn't it?

And I prove your precious theory.

'Juvenile Offender C', isn't that what you call me?

ANDY:—

SIMON: But what would happen to your reputation, your academic research if 'Juvenile Offender C' didn't prove to be rehabilitated?

ANDY: Well that's not what's happened.

SIMON: If I did it again?

ANDY: You won't. You understand the consequences.

SIMON: Do you believe that,

Or do you just want me to prove that your work was successful?

What if I lurked around where little Denis Pritchard lived? Grabbed
him? Covered his mouth and stuffed him in my duffle bag?

ANDY: I know you're testing me Simon.

SIMON: Easy to bury a child in the bush,
Isn't that what they're all saying around here?
I know that bush like the back of my fucking hand.
Wasn't it you who got me that job there—national parks and
wildlife—not near children, not near schools—quiet.
'He loves outdoors.'

ANDY: I know you're trying to undermine me.

SIMON: Stop it!
Can you be completely sure I didn't do it?
Because…
Don't forget I took a boy to a construction site and with my friends
I stood him there.
Watched him cry?

ANDY: Your friends weren't really your friends, remember?
Just boys from the streets.
And you were the youngest, Simon.

SIMON: Not by much.

ANDY: You were the youngest, a gang of street children.
There's a group dynamic.

SIMON: A group dynamic? Nice theory.
Why do you really make all these extra trips to see me?

Beat.

Your husband doesn't talk to you like I do, does he? /

ANDY: A group dynamic stops individuals acting as they normally /
would.

SIMON: You want to believe that I had the urge to run away from the
violence.
Believe that I wasn't so bad,
Because then it's okay to like me, isn't it?

ANDY: I believe you wanted to run away but /—

SIMON: But I don't, do I?

ANDY: Acting on the impulses of others.

SIMON: I stay and

I do it.

ANDY: As the victim's distress increases the tension and fear between the gang members increases.

Simon what you did was reprehensible.

But you were a child.

And you were told to do it.

SIMON: You say.

ANDY: I believe you just followed.

SIMON:—

ANDY: I believe you just followed.

SIMON: But you don't know.

ANDY: We'll never know.

SIMON: Unless I do it again.

Or I've done it again.

ANDY: You won't do it again.

Long beat.

SIMON: I just want to be normal.

ANDY: Then just be Simon Fontaine.

SIMON: I don't know him.

Who is he?

ANDY: I know him.

More than I know anyone else.

I know you completely.

SIMON: Is that allowed?

Beat.

Jessica wanted me to be Santa at her Christmas work party.

I got dressed up in that Santa suit.

ANDY: But you didn't go through with it.

SIMON: Maybe I did. /

ANDY: You know what's at stake.

If I breach you. And I could if you'd done that.

You go back to prison.

SIMON: But you wouldn't breach me?

ANDY: I don't want to breach you, but I would have no choice.

I would never lie to the Department.

There are rules.

No unsupervised contact with children.
No disclosure of true identity.
No dishonesty with me. /

SIMON *goes through the last lines of Andy's 'mantra' while she says it, he knows it so well, has heard it so often.*

SIMON: Jess wants a baby.

Beat.

ANDY: You can't let that happen.

SIMON: Why?

ANDY: We've been over this. You would require constant supervision and that would compromise your new identity.

SIMON: But, if Jessica knew why, she would understand.
She wouldn't tell a soul. I'd only need supervision when she wasn't there.

ANDY: I believe the stress of it would be counterproductive to your rehabilitation.

SIMON: But you can't stop me, can you?

ANDY: No.
But I would be expected to write a report about how it would compromise your rehabilitation.

SIMON: I'm not just your experiment.

ANDY: But you know I'm right.
I don't want you to fail.

SIMON: No babies.

ANDY: No.

SIMON: So let me tell her why.

ANDY: Tell her what?

SIMON: Something real.
I need to be honest with her.

ANDY: We need to keep this secret to protect you
From the media, from the public—
To protect you, and to protect Jessica /—

SIMON: Protect?

ANDY: We've constructed this life. We're in this together. You and me.
Listen to me, otherwise you're back in prison.
You tell Jessica and you've breached your parole.

That's my rehabilitation theory shot and you in prison.

Beat.

And—

Anyway, she wouldn't stay.

SIMON: She loves me.

ANDY: [*quietly*] Simon, you killed a baby.

It doesn't matter how old you were.

No woman would stay.

JESSICA *appears, looking around the squash courts.*

SIMON *and* ANDY *are unaware of her presence.* SIMON *puts his head in his hands, and* ANDY *after some hesitation, puts her arm around him.*

JESSICA *sees this and exits.*

SCENE FOURTEEN

JESSICA *sits in candlelight.*

LACHLAN *is broadcasting on the radio.*

LACHLAN: Volunteers from the district are joining police, emergency crew and staff from the National Parks and Wildlife in a fully orchestrated search combing outlying bush areas for the missing toddler Denis Pritchard, last seen in his back garden. Police have been recruited from Specialist Task Forces in an attempt to bring the child home safely.

Grave fears are now held as to whether the toddler could survive such heat and isolation after so many days. The child's mother is sedated and being supported by neighbours and family. The search continues throughout the night. This is Lachlan Cooper reporting for Radio Six.

SIMON *arrives home.* JESSICA *is asking questions with a tone that unnerves* SIMON, *though he doesn't know why.*

JESSICA: Did you win squash?

SIMON: No.

JESSICA: Andy played good hey?

SIMON: Yeah, sure did.

JESSICA: *He* was in good form?

Andy?

SIMON: Yeah.

JESSICA: You've never invited *him* over?

SIMON: Andy's just a squash mate.

SIMON:—

JESSICA:—

SIMON: You wanna eat out tonight?

JESSICA:—

SIMON: Italian, or something Asian?

JESSICA: I know.

SIMON:—

JESSICA: [*sarcastically quoting him*] 'I could never look at another woman.'

SIMON: What? /

JESSICA: You're having an affair, aren't you?

SIMON: What?

JESSICA: I came down to the squash courts.

SIMON: You went—

> *Beat.*

You checked up on me?

JESSICA: I had something to / tell you.

SIMON: You checked up on me.

JESSICA: I saw her!

Who is she?

SIMON: Don't you fucking trust me?

JESSICA: As it turns out maybe I shouldn't.

Just tell me—who is she?

I need the truth.

SIMON: Jess she's no-one.

JESSICA: Do you love her?

Because if you do—

Look at me, and tell me the truth.

Do you love her? /

SIMON: You have it all wrong.

JESSICA: Tell me!

SIMON: Andy. She is Andy.

JESSICA: You said she was a man.

SIMON: You assumed /—

JESSICA: Tell me the truth Simon,

How long have you been fucking her?

SIMON: Jess. No.

I just talk to her.

JESSICA:—?

SIMON: It's private.

JESSICA: Private!?

SIMON: She's a psychologist.

JESSICA: A psychologist!

You were at *squash*. I saw you.

SIMON: It makes it easier to talk.

She just bent the rules a bit.

Jess, I love you. You.

JESSICA: You never said you saw a psychologist.

SIMON: I'm not supposed to talk about it. I'm okay. It helps.

JESSICA: So what do you talk about? Me?

SIMON: No. Yeah. You, work. Everything.

My past. Childhood stuff.

JESSICA: About your stepfather?

> SIMON *nods.*

Did he do more than the broken arm?

Oh babe, did he—?

SIMON: I'm tired Jess,

It's—

I'm trying—

I want to be someone worthy of you.

A worthy husband.

But /—

JESSICA: You already are.

SIMON: No. No Jess.

I'm not.

JESSICA: You are!

And more than that my love.

A worthy father-to-be.

SIMON: Not now Jess. /

JESSICA: I rushed there to the courts to tell you something.

SIMON:—

JESSICA: As soon as the test came through.

SIMON: But you're on the pill!

JESSICA: I must have missed a few days.

SIMON:—

JESSICA: You're happy aren't you, for us?
A baby!

SIMON: But we said not yet.

JESSICA: What are you saying?
I'm not getting rid of it!

SIMON: We're not ready.

JESSICA: I am.
Simon, tell me you're happy about this.

Beat.

SIMON: [*very, very unsure*] Yes, yes.
Yes of course I am.

JESSICA: I knew you would be when it happened.

She embraces a stunned SIMON.

The door is banged loudly.

CAMILLE: Simon, Jess, it's Camille.
The search party.
They found something.
A shoe belonging to the Pritchard child.
It's in our patch.
The police are all over it.
Searching.
Matt wants our team there
You have to come in to work.
With me.
Now.

SIMON *grabs his forestry coat at the door and leaves.*

END OF ACT ONE

ACT TWO

SCENE ONE

Very late, after the search.

CAMILLE *and* SIMON *drinking beer.*

They drinking outside in the bush near their work headquarters.

CAMILLE *is slightly drunk.*

Their shift is over.

It's hot.

CAMILLE: I should feel more.
SIMON: Sometimes it's easier not to… /
CAMILLE: Do you feel more, or can you block it out?
SIMON: It's been a shit night.
CAMILLE: All that searching and nothing else.
 Not another sign of him.
 Where the fuck is he?
 It was our patch Simon, yours and mine.
 Makes me shudder.
SIMON: You should be home.
CAMILLE: No.
 Definitely not.
 Not the answer.
SIMON: Truth is you should go, Camille.
CAMILLE: The truth.
 Who wants the damn truth?
SIMON: Come on.
 I'll drive you.
CAMILLE: Me.
 That's who wants it.
 Without the truth, what are we Simon?
 Simon? What are we? Go on then, what?

SIMON: I don't know.
We're all just trying to get by.
CAMILLE: I don't believe you.
You don't believe that.
SIMON: Let's go.
CAMILLE: Without the truth we're just animals.
Like the prick who lured the boy out here.
That's what we are. /
SIMON: No. /
CAMILLE: Just lying stinking animals.
All of us. /
SIMON: You're drunk. /
CAMILLE: Aren't we? Aren't we all? /
You, even you. Aren't we?
SIMON: Okay yes.
Without the truth we are just lying stinking animals
You happy?
CAMILLE: Yes.
You bastard.

> CAMILLE *laughs.*

> *He reaches out to throw his arm around her, an act of drunken camaraderie.*

So now you want to fuck me?
SIMON: No. Of course not. /
CAMILLE: Because that would be a nice twist wouldn't it?
My husband is trying to fuck your wife and you're trying to fuck me.

> *Beat.*

SIMON: You've drunk way too much.
CAMILLE: I've seen him reach out for her.
I see it in his eyes.
SIMON: Jess would never. /
CAMILLE: Never?
SIMON: Go home Camille.
CAMILLE: I'm waiting here for Matt.

The poor little boy.
I try.
I try so hard.

   Beat.

I try Simon.
But I just can't make myself feel it.
SIMON: Feel what?
CAMILLE: I try. I pretend.
But Lachlan knows.
Angus knows.
Do you think I'm a monster?
SIMON: Yeah tonight you are a bit of a monster actually!
CAMILLE: I have these thoughts.
These terrible thoughts.
SIMON: What thoughts?
CAMILLE: That something will happen.
That I could hurt Angus.
That I could do something horrible.
SIMON: You'd never hurt him, Camille.
You're his mother.
CAMILLE: He's already a stranger to me.
I should have left before, before Angus.
We were broken already.
I knew then. Knew I couldn't do it.
But fucking Lachlan—
So desperate to be a father.
SIMON: I'm sure it's just a bad / phase.
CAMILLE: No.
It's all wrong Simon.
Everything.
Life's too short.

   Beat.

Will you listen Simon?
If I tell you something.
SIMON: Of course.
CAMILLE: You can't tell a soul.

Not even Jess.

SIMON: What is it?

CAMILLE: I need you to promise.

SIMON: Has something happened?

Okay, yes I promise.

CAMILLE: Simon I don't feel anything. Not properly.

For Angus.

No love.

Nothing.

I'm tired of failing.

SIMON: You don't love him; you don't love your baby?

CAMILLE: I don't know how to love either of them.

Not Angus.

And not Lachlan, anymore.

I just feel empty.

I'm a terrible, terrible person.

SIMON: No you're not.

CAMILLE: I'm fucking Matt.

SIMON:—

CAMILLE: I'm completely horrible.

SIMON: No.

CAMILLE: Tell me I'm a bitch. Go on.

Tell me I don't deserve Angus.

Tell me they're better off without me.

Go on tell me.

SIMON: You're a bitch.

You don't deserve Angus.

They'd be better off without you.

Better?

She laughs.

CAMILLE: No.

SIMON: You're a terrible monster, a fucking evil witch.

CAMILLE: Go on more.

SIMON: You're a—

You're a filthy whore, a stupid worthless piece of shit.

CAMILLE: A useless little tramp.

SIMON: A precious fucking cunt.

> CAMILLE *cheers.*

But you can look someone in the eye, a real person from your real
life and tell the truth.
For that I admire you.

CAMILLE: Yeah.

But I should be telling the truth to those who need to hear it.

SIMON: No.
I don't—
You just—
You just tell who you can tell.

CAMILLE: Thanks.

> *Beat.*

How does one little decision make it all such a fucking mess?

> *Beat.*

I wish I could talk to Lachlan like I can talk to you. We've lost that.
You're not really here if you can't share who you are.

SIMON: Do you believe that?
Do you—
Do you think—?
Do you think I'm really here Camille?

> *Beat.*

Can I tell you something too?
Promise me you won't tell anybody? /

CAMILLE: Oh God! /

SIMON: What? /

CAMILLE: Don't tell me you're fucking Matt as well!

> *She laughs.*

I promise. I promise on your promise.

SIMON: Something bad happened in my life. A long long time ago.
I [*He hesitates.*] made a mistake, a bad one, and I had to—
I changed my name.

CAMILLE: You're kidding me. You've got another name?
So what is it? The real one.

SIMON: You want to actually know the name?
CAMILLE: You trust me don't you?
SIMON: Yeah.
CAMILLE: So tell me.

> *Beat.*

> Promise I won't tell—
> I promise on Angus' life.
> Go on, what was it?

SIMON:—
CAMILLE: Harvey, no.
> Lucas?
> I know. I know.

> *She laughs*

> Ignatius.

> *Pause.*

SIMON: Richard.
CAMILLE: Oh? Richard.

SCENE TWO

Much later that night.

SIMON: You should be in bed.
JESSICA: Didn't find him?
SIMON: Nothing.
JESSICA: Did you drop Camille off?

> SIMON *nods.*

> Lachie came over, with Angus.
> Neither of you had your phones on.
> We were worried.

SIMON: Lachlan came over.
> Sounds convenient.

> *Beat.*

JESSICA: Actually Simon, it was.
> The police came around.

They wanted to talk to you.
Ask you questions.
Why Simon?
SIMON: Probably about the search.
JESSICA: But why come round here'?
What's going on?
SIMON: They're probably interviewing everyone.
JESSICA: But they were asking all sorts of questions
About you.
SIMON: It's probably a traffic thing, a speeding fine.
JESSICA: No.
Definitely not a traffic thing.
SIMON: What did they want?
JESSICA: They wanted to know things about your past.
SIMON: My past. What did you tell them?
JESSICA: Nothing. I don't know anything.
Only that you were taken away as a child.
SIMON: What? Why did you tell them that?
JESSICA: Simon why are you being—? /
SIMON: What else did you tell them?
JESSICA: Simon, where were you taken as a child?

> *Pause.*

SIMON: Jess, I was a messed up kid. I want all that behind me.
JESSICA: You said it wasn't a foster home.
Where were you taken?
SIMON: It was an, an institution.
JESSICA: Did you—
God, did you go to prison!?
SIMON: No. No.
Juvenile detention.
JESSICA: Oh my God.
SIMON: I was young.
JESSICA: What did you do?
SIMON: Just stealing and car stuff.
JESSICA: They put you in detention for that?
SIMON: I told you I was messed up.

JESSICA: Does Andy know?
SIMON: Yes.
JESSICA: How?
SIMON: I told her.
JESSICA: But not me.

> *Beat.*

SIMON: So now you tell me.
JESSICA: Tell you what?
SIMON: Do you think that without the truth we're just animals?
> Do you, Jess?
> Do you fancy him?
> Lachlan. /
JESSICA: Don't be stupid.
SIMON: Because he fancies you, doesn't he?
JESSICA: Don't.
SIMON: What?
JESSICA: Just trust me.
SIMON: He wants you, doesn't he?
JESSICA: He's vulnerable.
SIMON: Vulnerable!
> Is that what you call it? /
JESSICA: Okay, he likes me.
SIMON: Do you 'like' him?
JESSICA: Stop it.
SIMON: Are you fucking him?

> JESSICA *gives him a hateful look and goes to leave.*

See, you don't even need to answer.

> *He puts his arms around the back of her head, looks into her confused face.*

Because *I* trust *you.*

SCENE THREE

SIMON *barges into* ANDY's *inner city office.*

SIMON: They came to my house.

In uniform! /
They spoke to my wife.
They spoke to Jess.

ANDY: I know this must be terrible for you.
I've spoken to them.
It won't happen again.
It was a mistake.

SIMON: *A mistake!*

ANDY: They were just local cops.

SIMON: Why were they there?

ANDY: Simon they're investigating a missing child case.

SIMON: So what are you saying?
They're investigating *me!*

ANDY: They have to rule you out,
That's all.
You work in the area where they found the child's shoe!
Now, I have a client coming in, you have to go.

SIMON: They won't think that's a coincidence!

ANDY: Calm down.

SIMON: I'm the perfect suspect, aren't I?

ANDY: They'll follow procedure and rule you out.
I know you didn't do this Simon.

SIMON: How do you know?

ANDY: I know.
I understand you.

SIMON: What? What do you understand?
Tell me!

ANDY: I understand you are not that ten-year-old boy anymore and
I know that you understand that to lie to me is to lie to society.
And I know you don't want to do that.
Now go home, back to the life you've built.
Stay calm, continue to maintain your new identity, and I'll speak to
the Inspector allocated to your case about a safe time to interview
you.

    Beat.

Go.

SCENE FOUR

Christmas Eve.

LACHLAN *is at* JESSICA*'s place.*

There is a plastic Christmas tree with decorations.

LACHLAN: If he wakes up it usually means he's thirsty.
    Give him the bottle in the fridge.
    And then just pat him back to sleep.
    Thanks for this Jess.
    You're wonderful.
JESSICA: Mummy in training.

    LACHLAN *makes to go and then turns back.*

LACHLAN: I'm sorry I couldn't help with the trunk!
    It's locked tight.
    I'm sure
    Simon'll get it open. /
JESSICA: No. No. I don't want to tell Simon I lost the key.
    Okay?
    He'll think I'm so—
    I don't know,
    Don't say anything, will you?

    Beat.

    Lachlan.
    I'm worried—
LACHLAN:—
JESSICA: I'm worried you'll be late.
    Go, make things better.

    LACHLAN *kisses her.*

    SIMON *enters. He is wearing his uniform.*

SIMON: Not interrupting I hope!
LACHLAN: Just heard congratulations are in order.
SIMON: Okay. Thanks.

    SIMON *doesn't trust him.*

LACHLAN *leaves.*

What was he doing here?

JESSICA: Shh. We're babysitting Angus.

He's sleeping.

SIMON: Angus is here?

JESSICA: Lachlan packed a Christmas Eve picnic

For him and Camille.

They're having a rough time.

And he—

Champagne,

Candles.

All romantic.

SIMON: But Camille's still at work.

She's working… late.

JESSICA: Not for long!

Lachie's gone to surprise her.

SIMON: Surprise her?

He shouldn't do that.

> JESSICA *gives him a look.*

He just shouldn't.

JESSICA: Why?

> *The sound of a child calling.*

Oh God, there's Angus.

> SIMON *calls* CAMILLE'*s mobile and is frustrated when he obviously gets the message bank. He leaves a message. He doesn't see* JESSICA *return. She listens to his message.*

SIMON: Camille.

Um Lachlan is on his way over there.

To surprise you.

I just thought, I don't know, you and Matt should probably be warned.

> *He turns and sees* JESSICA *standing behind him.*

JESSICA: Why should Camille and Matt be warned?

SIMON:—

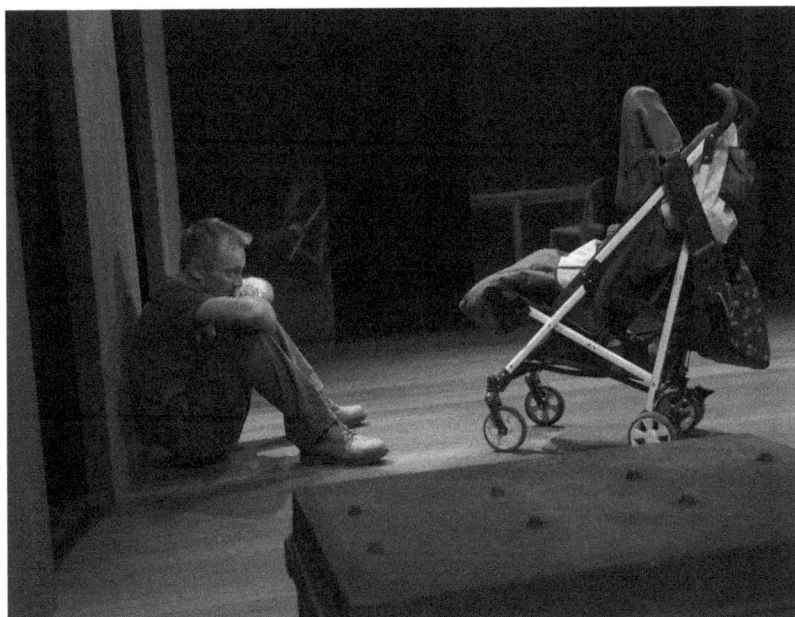

Richard Dormer as Simon in the 2009 Ransom Theatre production. (Photo: Rosie Mac Photography.)

JESSICA: Don't bother answering, it's obvious.

SIMON:—

JESSICA: Angus' drink is in the fridge; if he wakes up again you have to pat him back to sleep.

SIMON: You can't leave Angus with me.

JESSICA: It was my stupid idea that he go there.
I'm not letting him face that alone.

SIMON: Jess you can't.
No Jess. Please.

> JESSICA *leaves without looking back and Angus cries.*

> SIMON *stands still. The crying reaches a loud pitch.*

> *Shadows as* SIMON *finally makes his way to the where the child is sleeping.*

SCENE FIVE

LACHLAN *and* JESSICA *return to the house.* SIMON *is sitting next to the stroller and is gently singing and patting Angus.* LACHLAN *walks in first.*

SIMON: [*whispering*] He's asleep.

LACHLAN: You knew all along about them.
Didn't you?
Who are you?
Police at your door.
Helping your workmates secretly fuck each other.
I thought we were friends Simon.
I'm taking Angus.
We're going home.

> LACHLAN *exits with Angus.*

JESSICA: They were together.
All over each other.

SIMON: I sat with Angus while he had his drink, he was so sweet.
At one stage Jess he wanted a cuddle.
I cuddled his little body on my shoulder.

JESSICA: I yelled at her—
Told her Lachlan deserved better.

SIMON: Like a little koala.

JESSICA: That he deserved the truth.

SIMON: Let me hold you.

JESSICA: That we all deserved the truth in our lives.

SIMON: Let me touch our baby.

JESSICA: And do you know what she said?
That I was a fool,
That no-one ever knows the whole truth about anyone.
I told her she was wrong.
That I know you completely.
She looks at me hard and cold
And before she walks away she whispers
'Ask your husband who Richard is'.
And I don't know.
I don't know a Richard.
Do you?

SIMON:—

JESSICA: Do you know?
Who is he?
I'm asking you, Simon.

SIMON:—

JESSICA: Who's Richard? /

SIMON: Kiss me Jess /

JESSICA: Who is Richard?
Simon?

SIMON:—

He goes over and tries to hold her, to calm her.

JESSICA: Are you going to tell me?

SIMON: Jess, I can't. /

JESSICA *pushes him away.*

JESSICA: I have to know.
Tell me or I'll leave.

SIMON: It's me! Wait!

A long uncomfortable moment. SIMON *goes and gets the trunk, bringing it to* JESSICA.

He gets out a key and hands it to her.

You can't break the lock.

But you already know that.

[*Sadly*] Don't you?

> JESSICA *hesitates, takes the key.*

SCENE SIX

JESSICA *is at Simon's trunk, she approaches it and opens it.*

LACHLAN, *in earphones, reads the news announcement.*

LACHLAN: The town is gathered for a candlelight Christmas Eve vigil amidst fading hope of seeing little Denis Pritchard alive again. With Christmas only hours away, his mother is distraught.
Police say they have fresh leads in the case and are investigating around the clock.

> JESSICA *takes out the toys and starts to smile, she looks at the children's clothes. She lays them out, as if in preparation for someone.*

> SIMON *enters and* JESSICA *continues to sort through and lay out the clothes.*

JESSICA: What's all this stuff?

> *Beat.*

Is it for our baby?

> SIMON *shakes his head.*

Is it from when you were young?

But it's all new.

So—

I don't understand.

What's this got to do with your name being Richard?

SIMON: I collect it.

JESSICA: You collect kid's clothes—

Why? /

SIMON: I don't know why. It just feels right to do it.

JESSICA *is confused.*

    I collect it for him.

JESSICA: Him?

SIMON: Jess, the crime.

    When I was a kid.

JESSICA: What about it?

SIMON: There was a little boy—a two-year-old.

JESSICA: I don't understand.

SIMON: He was killed.

JESSICA: What?

SIMON: The stuff is for him.

    She drops the stuff on the ground.

JESSICA: Did you know him—the two-year-old?

SIMON: No.

JESSICA: So?

    I don't get it?

    Did you know his family? /

SIMON: It was a group of boys.

JESSICA: That's fucking awful Simon.

SIMON: One of the boys,

    His name was Richard.

    Back then.

JESSICA: Richard?

    Simon?

SIMON: I've wanted to tell you.

JESSICA: What are you telling me?

    No. I don't believe you.

    Why are you scaring me—

    You're lying.

    He goes to kiss her.

    She's crying but she responds slightly then violently pulls away
    and tries to undo the kiss.

    You killed a little boy?

SIMON: Yes.

JESSICA: No. You couldn't have—

SIMON: Yes.

JESSICA: No. I would have known.

SIMON: I was ten years old.

JESSICA: You're saying you're a child murderer.
That's why you were in prison.

SIMON: Juvenile Detention.
Till I turned eighteen.

JESSICA: You killed a baby boy.

SIMON:—

JESSICA: And you never told me.
You owed me.
I loved you.

SIMON: Loved?
No Jess don't say—
I would've told you—
But—
Andy—
She said I'd lose you.

JESSICA: I have poured all of my love into us
And it's all fake.
I've poured my love into a void.
I trusted you.
My God. I'm pregnant.
Simon!
Richard?
Who are you?

SIMON: I was ten.
You know me—
You know who I am.
You've lived with me all this time.

JESSICA: God what about the missing Pritchard boy?
Tell me you didn't go near him.
Oh God. Did you /—

SIMON: [*wounded to be asked*] No.

He tries to touch her but she hits him away.

JESSICA: Don't you come near me.

You murdered a baby.
You!
Tell me what you did,
Tell me.
I want the truth.

SIMON: [*angry and distraught*] You want to know what I fucking did?
Okay then—you want to know it all?
My job was to hold him down.
Restrain him.
Take his little body and keep it still
So they could do it to him.
And I held him down
Restrained him so he couldn't get away.
He can't move, and I hold him down hard.
To get it right.
When he cries I don't stop.
I tell him to 'be quiet'.
That's my job to hold him still.
And there are rocks for us there, rocks for us to hit his soft tiny head with,
And it only takes two hits to stop the crying,
But there are more hits than that.
Because we all know how to hit, all us boys,
We all know about hitting, and it feels good.
To do it.
We're all glad that it's quiet now.
Glad the noise of crying has stopped.
I held him down, and I liked that I was
Stronger than he was.
For once, I was stronger.
And I remember the feeling afterwards.
Knowing that the other boys
Liked me.
And I liked it.
So Jess
You know everything.
Are you happy now?

JESSICA:—

> JESSICA *leaves.*

SCENE SEVEN

ANDY's *office in the city.*

JESSICA *barges in.*

JESSICA: You know my husband.
> And my husband has been keeping secrets from me.

ANDY: I can't talk to you about any of my clients.

JESSICA: Oh I think you can.
> I've caught the train up here to your glamorous office
> especially to talk to you.

ANDY: You'll have to leave.

JESSICA: Before we were married he did something terrible and—
> Well I never knew anything about it.

ANDY:—

JESSICA: This terrible thing,
> He's famous for it

ANDY: Go on.

JESSICA: It's not a little thing either it's something big,
> Isn't it Andy? /

ANDY:—

JESSICA: Why was I not told?
> No-one told me,
> Not him, not the government.
> Not *you.*

ANDY:—

JESSICA: Jessica Fontaine,
> Although it's all just fiction really isn't it?
> I'm Simon's wife.
> Or am I Richard's wife?

ANDY:—

JESSICA: I want to know.
> Know why—
> Tell me why. /

ANDY: I'm going to ask you a question Jessica,
  And you must be very careful how you answer it. /
JESSICA: Okay / but—
ANDY: Don't say anything further until I'm finished.
  Jessica, if Simon has ever told you anything,
  Anything at all,
  That makes you doubt his identity
  I will have no choice but to breach him.
  That is my job.
  And just so you know,
  If I breach him he stands to serve all that is left of his sentence
  behind bars.
  Now I imagine that if Simon has kept to the rules of his parole,
  And not told anyone anything,
  Then in fact you probably think what I'm saying is very strange.
  Very strange indeed,
  In fact
  You probably think any talk of a parole or whatever,
  Is me talking about the wrong client.
  So
  If you know anything other than—
  Well of course you are obliged to tell me.

      Silence.

JESSICA: So…
  If Simon told me anything
  He knew he'd have to go to prison.
  And not see me again.
ANDY: Yes!
JESSICA: So by telling me he—
ANDY: *If!*
JESSICA: *If* he told me he would know that he was giving me something
  he wasn't allowed to?
ANDY: Yes!
  No matter how much he might want to tell you everything
  He knows the risk.
  If he told you.

JESSICA *nods and exits.*

SCENE EIGHT

CAMILLE *and* LACHLAN.

Sitting on bench, not facing each other.

CAMILLE: When I was ten,
    My dad bought me the sweetest little kitten.
    Bobo.
    White and fluffy, and I loved her.
    Or should have.
    Birman pedigree indoor cat,
    With her own little cosy bed, and little pink kitty tray.
    Dad used to clean the litter,
    All I had to do was give her some biscuits at breakfast,
    And make sure all the doors were shut.
    Keep her inside.
    That's it.
    That's all.
    Only four weeks and three days old and
    Just a ball of blood stained white fluff.
    The driver kept saying, 'I'm so sorry, I'm so sorry'.
    But it wasn't—
    We had a funeral for her but I kept crying for weeks.
    Dad's telling the neighbours how sensitive I am,
    How sweetly I loved Bobo.
    But it wasn't really an accident.
    She scratched me and I—
    I put her outside.
    Out the front door.
    Deliberately.
    I was cross with her for hurting me.
    It was all my fault.

    Beat.

I tried to tell you—

I knew—
Knew that I couldn't.
LACHLAN: A baby isn't a cat!
CAMILLE: I'm telling you I can't take care of him.
LACHLAN: Of course you can.
You're just trying to justify
Your shoddy little affair.
This is not about Angus.
CAMILLE: Things before were so—
Balanced.
And now—
I keep failing
and you keep pretending.
I knew
I couldn't do it.
And I told you the truth,
But—
I did try.
I tried Lachlan.
I have tried
So
Hard.

LACHLAN *finally looks at her.*

LACHLAN: Tell that to your son.

He turns his back on her and leaves.

She stands alone.

SCENE NINE

ANDY *and* SIMON *are in squash gear.*

They sit outside the courts.

Between Christmas and New Year.

SIMON: Do I need a lawyer?
ANDY: No I'll be there.

You must remember throughout the process that only the inspector knows your real identity.
The interviewing officers know you as Simon Fontaine.
Only.

SIMON: Okay.

ANDY: You haven't said anything to Jessica?

SIMON: [*without hesitation*] Not a word.

ANDY: Everything okay? /

SIMON: Wonderful.

> *She knows the lie.*

ANDY: You've done well Simon. This was a real test for you.

SIMON: So I pass with flying colours, don't I?
Told no-one any details, only talk to you.
Keep my re-identity clean.

ANDY: Yes I'm really proud of our work.

> *Beat.*

SIMON: Do you remember on my file—
When I was in detention that—
I had to go outside to see a dental surgeon.

ANDY: Yes, your first mobility from detention.

SIMON: So much security.
I was twelve, and so scared.
Not of the surgery.

ANDY: Tell me.

SIMON: So scared that all the people who wanted me
Dead
Would see me on the street.
And I remember thinking that
The people on the street *should* come and get me because I deserved it.
I'm a bad kid.
I'm an evil person.
That I was born evil.

> *Beat.*

I just wanted to—
I still just want to give him my place.

ANDY *holds his hand. He looks and she drops it.*

ANDY: That was a critical part of your development of insight.
  The beginning of you learning about good versus bad,
  Honesty versus dishonesty.
  The beginning of who you have become.
SIMON: What if you're wrong about me now?
ANDY: I'm not wrong.
  I have no doubt that
  You have been successfully reintegrated and rehabilitated.

  SIMON *looks away briefly.*

SIMON: So how's Michael?
ANDY: Michael?
SIMON: You remember him, don't you?
ANDY: Not at the moment, no?
SIMON: Are you sure?

  ANDY *shrugs.*

  Michael.
  You know, your husband.
ANDY: Oh right.
  Yes. Michael.
  He's well.
  Busy but well.
SIMON: Wish him a happy new year for me, won't you?
  Oh. And your kids.

SCENE TEN

SIMON *is at his place.*

The radio plays music. The plastic Christmas tree from previous scenes has been knocked over.

The news comes on the radio. SIMON *stops what he is doing and listens.*

LACHLAN: [*voiceover*] In an intriguing turn of events, police have
  today announced the miracle recovery of tiny missing toddler Denis
  Pritchard.

The little boy was discovered in a makeshift bush hideaway having been abducted by his estranged biological father. The father was previously interviewed at a local police station and was dismissed as a suspect. He is now remanded in police custody.

Denis's mother is said to be overjoyed at having her son back. Following the ordeal little Denis is now safely home cuddling the huge blue bear Santa had left in his Christmas stocking!

SIMON *turns off the radio and contemplates for a moment.*

JESSICA *enters. She has not heard the announcement.*

SIMON: Jess.

He gazes at her, longingly, fearfully, hopefully.

JESSICA: Richard. /

SIMON: Simon. /

JESSICA: I have something to say to you.

SIMON: Okay.

JESSICA: And then I'm going to leave /—

SIMON: Jess.
    When I was holding Angus, I realised
    I saw that I could do it.
    Saw that it would be all right.
    I can do this.
    The law will require supervision
    But Jess please I know I will be all right.
    I'm ready, we can do this.

JESSICA: No.

SIMON: I'll have supervision,
    Prove that I can do it.
    You'll see /—

JESSICA: Listen to me!

SIMON:—

JESSICA: If you ever contact me again
    Me
    Or my baby when it comes
    I'll go straight to Andy.
    I'll tell her I know everything.
    I'll tell her you told me.

SIMON: Jess, look at me.
It's me.
JESSICA: You'll go straight to prison.
SIMON: Please, please.
Jessica—
JESSICA: What choice do I have?
Live with a murderer?
SIMON: I told you everything because I love you,
Because I wanted us to be real.
JESSICA: [*she laughs*] Real!
I'll tell you what's real?
You murdered a baby in cold blood.
And you let me love you.
You let me love you!
And now I'm pregnant with [*touching her belly*] this.
A child who could be /—
SIMON: Evil?
You think I'm evil?
Tell me you don't mean that.
JESSICA: You held him down.
You watched him die.
You did nothing to save him.
SIMON: [*agreeing sadly*] I know...

> *She starts laying into him, hitting him hard with her fists; he tries to fend off her punches.*

JESSICA: You tricked me into loving you, touching you.
Fucking you.
SIMON: Please Jess.

> *He holds her arms so she cannot hit him, restraining her for her own good.*

> *She struggles against him, and hits him over and over as she speaks.*

> SIMON *takes all the hits.*

JESSICA: You disgust me,
Everything about you,

Your lies, your secrets—
I feel sick.
You're a monster, a killer.
I despise you.
You disgust me.
And I disgust myself.
You make me feel sick,
Just to look at you.
Do you hear me?
You make me sick.
Just to look at you makes me sick.
Even as I fucking love you,
you make me feel sick.

> *She stops fighting him, goes still and silent. She is depleted and worn.*

SIMON: [*making a last honest attempt to convey who he is*] When they
mentioned him it would just come from nowhere,
The smell of him, the smell that is just his smell.
And I'd sit there in that cold stone courtroom, on a wooden bench.
All those strangers staring at me,
And the judge up there, like God.
And I'd think of him and remember his soft smell.
I'd always want to vomit, feel it rising—
But I never—
Instead, I'd count in my head.
Just numbers in my head.
Numbers to stop me remembering.
But it's always there.
Always.
There's a warmth spreading between us,
Our bodies so close.
But it's not blood,
It's the stinging heat of piss seeping over us both.

> *She backs away from him.*

And I don't know if it's him or it's me.
I'm ashamed, embarrassed, afraid.

Milk and fear and blood and piss, and a sweet smell that is us.

JESSICA goes to leave as SIMON *continues talking, opens the door, pauses at the door.*

If I look up in that stone courtroom, if I look just a little up
My mother is there. Alone. And she won't look at me.
I want her to look at me.
I want her to come over and hold my hand.
Like he wanted his mum to hold his hand.

She turns around.

She is crying but refuses to meet his eyes.

Just after the blood that's the moment I can smell.
Up close
His tiny body against mine,
And I can hear voices but not his
Not his crying anymore,
And I'm there.
Me.
I'm right there,
With him.

Her eyes rise to meet his. Eyes lock. Connected.

Pause.

Blackout.

THE END

www.ingramcontent.com/pod-product-compliance
Lightning Source LLC
Chambersburg PA
CBHW041932090426
42744CB00017B/2028